The Ultimate Girlfriend

CW01064421

How to Become Irresistible, Avoid Rejection and Get the Girls You Want

MATT BRADON

CONTENTS

DEDICATION ii

INTRODUCTION 5

PART ONE: GETTING YOURSELF ATTRACTIVE 1
1

CHAPTER ONE: Everything that Glitters is Gold 1
2

CHAPTER TWO: Will He Become the President 1
8

CHAPTER THREE: Hey, Be Nice but not too Nice 2
2

CHAPTER FOUR: Addicted to Power 2
7

PART: MAKING THE MOVE 3
3

CHAPTER FIVE: Put Her Under your Spell 3
4

CHAPTER SIX: Conversation: Say the right thing and Avoid 3
being Friend Zoned 7

CHAPTER SEVEN: How to Get Her Number and Things to 4
Avoid Saying 4

CHAPTER EIGHT: Making Use of the Signs of Attraction   50

CHAPTER NINE: The Best Place to Meet these Girls (Location, Location, Location)   58

CHAPTER TEN: Overcoming the Fear of Rejection   63

INTRODUCTION

Scenario 1

You see this beautiful girl you like. Since that day you've been consumed with her. When you eat, sleep and drink its her. And if you are currently schooling, you see her in your studies. You tell your friends about her, they give you a nod and encourage you to go ahead and talk to her. But you think what do I say, I don't want to annoy her? Does she like me? Heck, I don't want to be rejected. She even looked at you, is it a sign that you should go ahead and talk to her. You managed to introduce yourself to her, and for the next few days you worship her with attention, and you do almost anything she asks for. You asked her out and she blurted out no, or she said I thought we were just friends (if you ever actually got to this stage).

Scenario 2

Mike sees a girl for the first time, he thinks she's attractive, he makes up your mind to go talk to her. He is highly motivated as his buddies has told him he has to take risks. He decided to give it a shot. He introduced himself and asked her if she would like to take something. Mike splashes some cash to get her and her friends what they want. He told them all about himself and made a lot of jokes.He was excited to see them laugh at his jokes. At the end Mike asked for her number, she got angry and walked away with her friends. Mike sat there immobilized (Its a terrible place to be in).

This could happen to anyone. And maybe this isn't the first time its happening. It has happened so many times you've become emotionally demoralized. So what are these guys doing wrong. Why will she accept another guy, even a player who treats her badly, instead of you, a nice guy who would do anything for her. It turns out that you are missing something, something that bad guys and players know too well and are using to their advantage. You don't have to be a player or a mafia lord to attract as many girls as you want and actually go into a meaningful relationship with them. In fact the type of guys girls really want is a guy that will respect them, care for them and love them, all these qualities of which bad guys lack and still get away with it. In the chapters ahead we are going to see how you can get your self into a position where many and even most girls will find it difficult to say no to you by playing your cards the right way. I mentioned card because it is a game although more complex than those written by human programmers.

PERCEPTION

Success in dating isn't about who you really are on the inside (though very important, and even imperative in marriage). Its about how the opposite sex perceives you. And if you give them the right perception and attract them you've done a huge part of the job it takes to get them. Women will consider you very attractive if you are talking to a lady who is very attractive and has high social value, even if you are a nobody. They'll begin to wonder what you have that she's attracted to. If you want to succeed in dating, there's one thing you should always keep at the back of your mind:

Men care about how the package looks (is it beautiful, hot, youthful etc). all of which is superficial), but women care about what is perceived to be inside the package (he looks strong, he seems confident, other girls like him etc.) all of which are also superficial. You see, you can even conclude that we humans are superficial beings, but I'm not going that way. Girls care about what she thinks or what other people think is inside the package. It doesn't matter if there is nothing inside. As long as she feels there's something inside, you are all good.

PART ONE- MAKING YOURSELF ATTRACTIVE

Part one   is all about getting yourself attractive and irresistible, however if you feel like girls are already attracted to you and your biggest challenge is approaching them, you can jump straight to part two. The psychological magic in part two is most effective when girls already find you attractive. Before you approach a girl, you want to be the kind of guy that the girl will find attractive. Will she be happy to tell her friends, this is my boyfriend. Can she introduce you to to her parents and family members without feeling embarrassed (if they don't like you it shouldn't be because of something you can easily take care of). And if a girl is attracted to you, you've done up to 70% of the job of getting her. She will be thinking, I like this guy, how can I get him to notice me. Trust me, they'll give you a lot of signals. And if you can take note of them, bingo! You are very close to getting what you want. Getting her attracted to you is just a part of the job, and in fact the other part of the job is where most guys fail. Most guys fail at actually letting the girl they like know about their intentions. The second part of the book is going to deal with how to let her know about your feelings without being rejected. Well it's not like sometimes you are not going to be rejected but the rejection isn't going to look like one. As we will see later, It is easier to get a girl who is already interested in you than to get a girl who is not interested in you to develop interest in you, although it is by no means impossible. I'm going to show you a method any guy can use to get any girl. They are not even difficult to follow. It just requires you to make a little structural changes to your mind.

Getting them attracted to you is just like making a high quality product, you still have to convince them that its a high quality product and they should buy it- which is the subject of part two.

PSYCHOLOGICAL TRICKS

It's all about psychology. To get the girls you want or to get them to admire you, you are going to need some psychological tricks. How soon you can start using these tricks depend on how comfortable with them. As time goes on, you will surely become more comfortable with them. If you want to know the power of psychology, ask successful salesmen. To survive in the sales business you have to get into people's head and find out what they want and why they want it. That's what we are going to be doing here. We are going to travel into her mind to see what she really wants. You can never know what's in the mind of a particular girl, but you can have an idea of whats in the mind of girls in general. Once you know what these ladies want, your duty is to give it to them. It's not hard to do, with a little commitment on your part to learn, you can start living the dream.

The book is divided into two parts, the first part is about making yourself the kind of guy that girls are attracted to. But, attraction alone will not help you get her, you have to actually approach her. The problem is that you can't just approach her anyhow, the way you approach her will determine if you are accepted or you get one of those pink slips- which is the subject of part two.

PART ONE

GETTING ATTRACTIVE

I have removed some things that can make you attractive like being popular or handsome that you can do little or nothing about and focus on the ones you can do something about. And these ones happen to have the greatest impact.

CHAPTER 1

EVERYTHING THAT GLITTERS IS GOLD

YOUR LOOKS

Looking good gives you confidence. If people see you and what they see make them feel positive, they'll reflect that positivity back to you which will in turn increase your confidence. Its like a virtuous cycle. Looking good doesn't mean looking like Hulk or Brad Pitt, all you have to do is to look your best. While expensive and flamboyant dressing is sure to draw a lot of glances, you don't need to break the bank to look good or attractive. All you have to do is to maintain good hygiene and make sure you are comfortable with what you are putting on. Looking good can be something as simple as wearing clothes that fits, wearing color that complements each other and most importantly wear clothes that you feel comfortable in. Have you ever left home and discovered later that there was a little stain or a tear on your clothes? Even if no one would notice, chances are that it will bring down your confidence. You'll spend all day thinking, what if they notice? What if they've noticed it? Wearing the right clothes gives you confidence and keeps you in a positive mood. You also want to wear clothes that are in fashion or not too far away. Looking good is also about keeping yourself cleanly shaven and brushing your hair. As many girls would say some muscles on him doesn't hurt. Building some muscles and looking physically fit is very sexy to girls. It make you look strong and girls like guys that are strong because they feel safe around them. Muscles make you look attractive up to a limit. Some boys seeing that girls like muscular guys take muscle building to the extreme. They end up looking like monsters who most girls are actually afraid of. Looking good is simple, but it doesn't mean strange. Most geeks think that there are infinite things more important in the universe than their appearance, as a result they end up neglecting their appearance. If you are a geek, you might want to work on your appearance. If looking like a geek is more important to you than getting the girl you want, you are going to struggle to attract them. Geeks usually find success with women later in life. And then its because they've become successful (they now have money or a good career) and they've learnt to adjust to fit in somehow.

MAKING USE OF SCENTS

Some years back I attended a seminar. In this seminar I happened to be sited next to a lady. Now some few minutes later a guy came a took a sit beside me. I have to say the first thing I noticed was the irresistible fragrance that was following him. As this guy sat he literally changed the atmosphere around us. The fragrance did smell good to me but as I have nothing for guys it didn't mean much to me. But the lady beside me tried in vain to control herself. She had to give this guy a lustful stare. Of course, she didn't know I was seeing her. Even if she knew, she just couldn't help herself. Good fragrance can make anyone feel good and if you are interested in the person it can prime them up , help reduce their guard and make it easy for you to approach them. It can sometimes spark conversation, if the person likes the way you smell. Like " wow I like the scent of that pefume, what's the name etc." Again your perfume doesn't have to be the most expensive or even expensive at all. Just choose something you like that smells nice.

CONFIDENCE

Confidence is not the absence of fear, the absence of fear is ignorance. Confidence for me is the ability to do what you know you should do even in the presence of fear. You are afraid of the outcome of a job interview but yet you pick up the courage to do it, that's confidence. Nothing gives you more confidence than getting your life in order. You can do this by setting goals for yourself and achieving them and having a general plan for your life. It can be doing some difficult stuff or having something important going on in your life. You need to show these girls that you have your own life, that you can defend your self and her too if need be. You need to show her that you can stand your ground when the inevitable problems of life show up. The way you look, being in a good shape and smell can help your confidence a lot. The more confidence you have, the less you care about rejection, and the less you care about rejection the more women you'll get. Its like a virtuous cycle. And you can kick start that cycle by changing the way you look. Looking good and in shape is mostly hard work and wearing clothes that fits. It doesn't to be expensive. In fact, if its expensive, you are trying too hard.   Confidence also means being willing to wait to get her or to even let her go. I got attracted to a newly employed girl in my work place. The girl was very attractive and some other guys including my friends were attracted to her too. Like all guys do, we were all trying to make the first move and register our intention and get her contact. I was afraid the other guys would get her before me, but because I know girls like to take things slowly I had to hold myself back. While I'm attracted to her I don't want to be begging her to be my girlfriend, if she doesn't want me then so be it. There are many other girls out there. Do not be in a hurry to approach a girl. As this might signal lack of confidence. You should make her feel like if she doesn't want you a million other girls are out there dying for your attention.

DUTCH COURAGE

It's sad that that many girls cannot tell the difference between real confidence and induced confidence. Many assholes are every bit as afraid of rejection as you are, but they overcome their fears with alcohol and other substances. This can sometimes work against them as they become drunk and unable to control themselves. I do not personally advise anyone to go that route just because you want a girl. And if ever you do, do not become a drunkard or addicted. The saddest part of dutch courage is addiction. If you are not already there please do not go. I've been there. It's not the best place to be.

CHAPTER 2

WILL HE BECOME THE PRESIDENT

AMBITION

`

If you are still depending on your parents you sure might not have your own money. Having money is not not a problem for women as long as you have the potential to make it. That's when ambition comes in. What are you goals and what are you doing to achieve them? Why do you think girls are attracted to those who make it to the high school baseball or basketball team? Potential. Girls want to be with someone they think has a great future. Not just girls, I think everybody wants to be with someone one who has a great future. If the next Jeff Bezos or Bill Gates was in your high school class and you know it, wouldn't you want to be close to them. What ever talent you have, you better start putting it to use now. Be good at doing something. Not just anything, something that other people value. Of course being very good at playing video games is not sexy. Why? Because no one will pay you to play video games, no matter how good you are.

I had a friend who was part of a church choir. He was their drummer. When he plays on Sunday a camera zoom in on him for the very large congregation to see. On our way home after church service, we meet a lot of girls who say hi to him just because they saw him on the screen. So many girls want his attention that he treats them like diapers. He goes for another one every new month.

 When girls go into relationship, they are thinking about the long term. Even the ones that you say to 'let's just have some fun and everyone goes their way ', later gets emotionally involved. Even if your real motive of wanting the girl is short term, you have to think long term like her to be able to get her. Any thing you do to improve your life that others can notice will attract girls-even the ones you do not like for one reason or the other. Girl wants to be with the best of any thing. Some of them are surprising-the best armed robbers, assasins, mafia lord, the most popular guy, the best scientist etc. Once you are good at anything, it seems it doesn't matter if it's good or bad, girls will flock to you. In summary be good at something valuable. Just like you don't just want any girl you want a very attractive one. If you are only able to choose one thing from an many options, you want that thing to be the best. Biologically and socially, ladies are allowed to get one man or at most a few, but men have unlimited options or a very high limit (King Solomon had a thousand women). So you can't blame women for being very selective. Ladies want to be with the best guy around or the guys they think are going to be the best in the future. Working on to improve yourself shows you take on a lot of responsibilities and can take care of her. She's thinking will being with this guy make my life better. So assure her it will.

MONEY

Girls like to be treated like pets, who doesn't want to. When you have a lot of money girls can only imagine what they can do with it. If money is the only thing you have, you can be sure you won't have problem with girls. No matter how strange you look. Whether you are a geek or an introvert. In his book *How to Win At the Sport of Business*, Mark Cuban tells a story of how he got some insanely attractive girls ticket to a party. He went to get drinks for them, only to come back and find out the girls were gone. He later found out that it was Bill Gates who took his girls.

'As I would learn later in life', said Mark Cuban, *'money makes you extremely*

handsome.'

A nice high end car will get you a lot of attention. Wearing gold or high end shoes wristwatches will get you a lot of attention. However if someone is attracted to you because of your bling bling, that is probably what they are attracted to and not you. If you are rich, you can easily get laid, but do not expect to get something more meaningful than sex from these girls. Many that are attracted to you because of your riches are probably gold diggers or prostitutes. The good thing is that out of the plethora of girls that are attracted to your riches a few of them really like you, and might be ready to go into a relationship with you. Of course money is not going to help you ask these girls out. And sadly money is not going to shield you from rejection. You still have to learn how to do it the right way to avoid unnecessary rejections, which we shall see in part 2 of this book. Let me reiterate, money will get you laid, but it won't prevent rejections.

CHAPTER 3

HEY, BE NICE BUT NOT TOO NICE

DO NOT BE TOO CLINGY

Girls are human beings and not robots. As much as they want a guy in their life they do not want to have someone who cannot let them be free to live their own lives. They do not want someone who acts like a micro manager, following her everywhere. I had a friend who monitors every move his girlfriend made. In fact he became my friend because he wanted me to help him spy on his girlfriend. He always felt his girlfriend was doing something with someone else. She can't talk to other guys without him being jealous or suspicious, this guy was giving her rules like he was married to her. The girl ended up dumping him.   If you know you can't trust someone there no use making her your girlfriend. If you do, you are going to get a lot of heart break and heart attack.

Following a girl everywhere she goes won't prevent her from doing what she wants to do. If she was decent girl before you met her , she will likely remain a decent girl. If you go into a relationship with the intention of changing anyone, I'll say good luck. To avoid many future problems make sure you know the girl you are going into a relationship with.

YOU HAVE TO FIT IN SOCIALLY

Being unconventional might help you win the Nobel prize or make some technological breakthrough, but it's not going to do you much good in the dating world. Whether we admit it or not, most of the decisions we make are influenced by others. That is, we make decisions based on whether other people will like it, not based on merit. So, if in the social circle of a girl you like, they think you look awkward or you are too different, chances are that she'll want to avoid you. This is especially true of, but not limited to, those who consider themselves nerds and geeks. You want people in her social circle to having nothing bad to say about you. Or if they have something bad, they should have more good things to say about you. Or even better they should have nothing to say about you. If she likes you she'll be the one to shape their perception about you. You can be unconventional and still be able to attract girls, you just have to let that unconventionality reside in your head. On the outside you like like everyone else but on the inside you are way different and doing your own thing. There are some girls though that like unconventional guys, that's when you are popular for being unconventional, otherwise they are not much.

GET RID OF NEEDYNESS AND DESPERATION

You meet this girl, she's so beautiful, she the only thing that matters in the world. If you loose her to another guy you will die. So you go all attack even before the referee blows the whistle. But that's the wrong way to approach a girl and the sure path to rejection. Do not rush into asking a girl out because you are afraid you will loose her. In fact be prepared to loose her. An alarming percentage of marriages end up in divorce and these couples still go on to live their lives without the person they once loved. You can do without anything and if you can live without one of your kidneys I see no particular girl that you cannot live without. Having this in mind build the relationship at a pace that is comfortable for her. I know guys are ready to meet a girl today, propose to her, marry her and have kids on the same day. Only a prostitute would do that, and you would pay a premium price for it. But, most women are not like that and you should respect that. Well it's not anyone's fault- it's genetic.

Same thing happens in bed. Many guys go straight to the point and they arrive at their destination without the girl onboard. Well they think because they are seeing her she came with them. In fact she is lost and doesn't know what's going on. You feeling like you have done a marvelous job ask her, "honey how did I do". She being socially Intelligent massages your ego by telling you did better than Hercules. When it comes to women slow is fast, but many do not learn until they get burned with rejection that leaves them without self esteem. Do not come on too strong on girls especially those you are just getting to know. Desperation, in the form of trying get her by all means, like getting a girlfriend is the only thing that matters in your life is a huge turn off. If you come on too strong you loose that sense of secrecy, she already knows all you want is her. It becomes a common thing or normal thing that you like her and there's nothing special about that.

YOU TREAT THEM WITH RESPECT

 As bad as assholes are, they still manage to treat ladies with a lot of respect, at least until they are tired of her and have moved on to someone else. Even if you have to pretend to be nice to her, do it. I was at a friend's house when his sister came to ask us how she looked. My friend replied in the tune of "how did that affect him". I simply told her she looked great but could make some adjustments on her shirt. She told me thank you and I could see she felt great. My friend was obviously doing that because it was his sister, but being nice to your sister can teach you how to nice to other girls and help you know how to react to your praise and criticisms. Ladies like validation, even the hottest ones out there still want to be told that they are beautiful and look great. They don't get tired of hearing it just like they don't get tired of using a mirror to check out their looks. If she makes an effort to look different make sure you are one of the first to notice it and praise her. Girls find guys who can notice the effort they are making to look beautiful very sexy. Even when she isn't making any effort, just telling her she looks great will make her day. Treat them like queens but do not go too far with this. Treat them too nicely and they begin to take you for granted or it might seem pretentious to them. If a girl does something that obviously wrong, let her know but do not take it too serious. If you take it too serious she might think you hate her.

Why can't nice guys get girls? The answer is: because the only people they are nice to is girls. If you are pretending to be nice just to get a girl, they'll see through it. The ultimate test of how nice you are is not how you treat a girl, but how you treat the door man or those you despise. Guys really need to learn how to be nice, and it's simple- by treating the the people that comes your way with respect, irrespective of their status.

CHAPTER 4

ADDICTED TO POWER

Ladies will die to get men that are powerful. If there's one force that women can't resist on this planet it's power. No matter what a woman tells you, they like to be dominated. Being dominated is in fact one of the most common sexual fantasy of women. Now where does this power come from. Traditionally power comes from having a lot of money or being the one in control of a lot of resources. Yes, those things makes you powerful, but when it comes to relationship, the subtle type of power works best.

Robert Greene in his masterpiece 48 Laws of Power wrote about some powerful lessons on attraction in the 16th law. Here's one way you can weild power subtly from the book:

At the start of an affair, you need to heighten your presence in the eyes of the other. If you absent yourself too early, you may be forgotten. But once your lover's emotions are

34

engaged, and the feeling of love has crystallized, absence inflames and excites. Giving no reason for your absence excites even more: The other person assumes he or she is at fault. While you are away, the lover's imagination takes flight, and a stimulated imagination cannot help but make love grow stronger.

To play the power game in a relationship you have to make you partner feel that you are scarce and if they don't reciprocate you love you might leave them. One of my favorite songs portrays this: Passenger in his song *Let Her Go* said:

Only know you've been high when you're feeling low

Only hate the road when you're missing home

Only know your lover when you let her go.

The truth is that the way the human mind is built, it only appreciates what it has when it feels scarce or when it's gone. This is the reason why people don't appreciate the air they breath, even though we cannot survive a day without it. This is also why we may long to have our ex back, even though they caused a lot of trouble that led to your separation. Even girls have discovered this- if they accept a guy too easily, the guy sees them as cheap. So, ladies not wanting to look cheap, give guys a lot of heart ache before they accept them. That's why guys are one of the biggest reasons why women are difficult to get. They don't want to look cheap. Some guys seem not to mind this and in fact enjoy the adrenaline buzz that comes with chasing them.

When you meet a girl you are attracted to for the first time, what you have to do is to extablish a strong presence. Tease her, flirt with her, tell her sweet words, make her feel special. Then you withdraw suddenly and without warning. Even if she tries to reach you, ignore her text and calls for some time but not for too long unless she might forget about you. When the calls or texts have reduced totally then come back into here life. You have just killed her with attraction for you. I bet if a girl does it to you, you won't be able to resist it. No it's impossible. Money is loved because it is scarce. Learn how to withdraw from your lover to create scarcity. There is another way you can also create scarcity- by talking to other girls. I have blown the head of many girls using this method.

There was a very beautiful girl that was flirting with me in my place of work. I responded in kind by flirting with her also. She has a boyfriend whom I know. I was wondering why she was still flirting with me. I discovered it wasn't just me – she flirted with just about any guy. She also got whatever she wanted from guys- gifts, praise, attention, and she was worshiped like a god. She treated guys the way she liked, her boyfriend was no exception. I talked to her boyfriend and he seemed not to care, he said what he wants was her body and if he can get it he doesn't mind what she does. I had a few conversations and flirted with her. After a few weeks I stopped flirting with her and started talking to one other girl. She started evesdroppig on our conversation, she became jealous. She started questioning our conversation, she even went ahead to report me to the girl's boyfriend. I was amazed at why she'll do that, because I wasn't actually dating her. I was just flirting with her to let her know I was interested in her. Because she felt she was loosing me she became more attracted to me. I learnt one lesson that girls want what they cannot have.

GO FOR YOUNGER GIRLS

Ask your dad how he did with women as he got older. Hint: he will never tell you or he will feel awkward talking to you about it. Or if you are lucky to have that one in a million father he'd open up to you, if he feels it's the right time. Too bad parents do not have time or are just uninterested in teaching their kids the some of the most important things in life. Some parents will even scold their kid for thinking about relationships at their age. Even when you are not too young, even when you are very young these emotions are real. Your parents forgot that they they felt the same way when they were younger than you. Our memories are very short, although for a good reason.

Women in general tend to like older men. As men age they become more attractive to women. This is why even the guy that finds it difficult or impossible to have a girl friend when they were young are all married except the ones that choose not to. Even Bill Gates was rejected by a girl in high school, maybe because he was a geek, but now I can count the number of girls in the world that would reject Bill Gates on my palm. Even if you don't have to be a multi billionaire like Bill Gates, as you get older you become more attractive. Men become more financially secure as they age, they become more responsible and dependable. If there's anything that attracts a lady it is a finished product. The younger the woman you are trying to date, relative to your age, the more successful you'll be at getting her. Of course it is up to an extent, you don't expect a 20 year old girl to date an 80 year old man, except that they sometimes do. That's because women are the 8th wonder of the world.

PART 2

MAKING THE APPROACH

 Objects in mirror are closer than they appear- Side-view mirror.

CHAPTER 5

PUTTING HER UNDER YOUR SPELL

When you fall in love, you fall under a spell. You begin to do all sorts of things that the normal you would consider insane. Love and attraction is irrational, but evolution considers it the most rational thing on the planet. As long as something irrational will bring two people together to produce the next generation, Mr. Evolution is a happy man. If two people are under the spell of love, the person who can manage to reduce the effect of that spell holds the control button. This is where many guys get it wrong when approaching a girl, they hand over the control button to her. How do guys give girls the control button? If a girl likes guy, she's going to be coy about it, she's going to make you guess which is going to get even more crazy for her. Today she says hi, tomorrow she acts as if you do not exist. But, if a guy likes a girl, what does he do ? The exact opposite. The girl is going to know from a hundred miles away that he likes her. He's going to worship her with attention and will take anything from her including being treated like trash. He will become the nicest guy on the planet. He will do just about anything just to please her, and through all his actions he will become the most predictable robot on the planet. The result of this is that she will begin to say things like : 'we lack chemistry', ' he's not exciting', and many other excuses. Why ? That's because you have given your love away so easily and it has lost it's value.

That's why Arthur Schopenhauer said:

It is advisable to let everyone of your acquaintance- whether man or woman- feel now and then that you could very well dispense with their company. This will consolidate friendship. Nay, with most people there will be no harm in occasionally mixing a grain of disdain with your treatment of them; that will make them value your friendship all the more. ... But if we really think highly of a person, we should conceal it from him like a crime. This is not a very gratifying thing to do, but it is right. Why, a dog will not bear being treated too kindly, let alone a man!

I know some girls that said yes even before the guy asked them out. What usually follows is the guy telling his friends that the girl is cheap, in most cases the relationship doesn't last long. Even guys do not value the girls they can get easily, let alone girls. While you want to let her know that you are interested in her, you want to do it in a way that will leaving her wanting more. You want to make feel like if she doesn't want you, she can get the f*** off, there are many girls out there that wants you. No one is going to place more value on you than yourself. You let her know that she's your queen, your diamond, your everything etc, but if she takes you for granted you'll walk away. Even if if you know you can't walk away.

 When approaching a girl you should try to conceal your interest in her. Show her a glimpse of love for some time and then act as if there is nothing. While you keep her guessing, you will increase her fantasy and desire for you, until it gets to a point when she wants you more than you want her. Now I have to admit that concealing your intentions if you are attracted to someone as a guy is difficult. But, you can learn it by practicing and it's not too hard. The guys that do it gets almost any girl they want. A good way to do this is through your conversations with her. And that's what the next chapter is about: Using words to get her under your spell.

.

CHAPTER 6

CONVERSATION

Say the Right Thing and Avoid Being Friend Zoned

If you find it easy to talk with many people then girls shouldn't be any different. The only difference is the topic you choose to talk about. There are some topics that are universal that are not personal e.g. where you'd like to travel to and movies. To have more things to say you have to be cultured. This especially true for those STEM guys. If the only thing you want to talk about is some heavenly equations and some philosophical debates on the origin of man then you are going to have a hard time talking to many people, how much more girls. There are some topics such as politics or sports that guy's enjoy talking about that will bore girls.

The trick to having conversations and making connection with girls is to talk about what they are interested in. And if you are good at small talk, you are on the right path. Girls are mostly interested in talking about relationships, movies, gossips, shopping or travel experience and if you hear her singing a music, it will be a good topic to discuss with her.

But it is not the talkers that gets the women, it is the slick talkers. When you talk to women, make use of the subtle method. Those words like "I love you", "you are beautiful", etc. have been heard more than hundreds of times from more than hundreds of guys. Those word while can be effective sometimes have now become like a cliché to them. Look for new words to tell them they are special to you. And make sure you do not use same words on different girls if they are friends, because they are going to tell their friends what you said and that will most likely put you in their black list. If you do ever go for more than one girl at a time make sure they are not friends. You don't have to invent words to tell them. Many music out there are about love and you can copy them and modify it. Using speechless by Michael Jackson you can tell a girl she makes you feel speechless. Like a girl told me that the first time she met me she thought I couldn't talk. I told her she was the one that made me speechless. What followed was she blushing.

You should also direct the conversation towards what you want. If you are discussing music or travel or relationship with a girl, it's just a means to an end. Your main interest is her and not music or travel. To avoid being friend zoned, you should start chipping in your interest from the first conversation, but you have do do it subtly. For example, instead of just talking about music if she's into music, at some point in the conversation you can just chip in that you don't know why you like people that are into music or you've been looking for someone that knows a lot about music for a very long time. Trust me, they know what you mean. Even the thought of what you actually meant turns her on.

I met a girl I was attracted to sometime ago. On meeting the first time we just exchanged pleasantries, I told her my name and asked her about hers. She told me her name. I made sure the name sticked to my mind. The next time I met her, I called her name several times and made a joke about how I liked her name like this:

Me: Vanessa, Vanessa, how are you doing? I'm so happy to see you.

Vanessa: I'm fine. Good to see you too.

Me: Vanessa, I don't know why I like that name. I'm mean the name just gets me excited anytime I hear it.

Vanessa: (She laughs)

Me: Well, I think I going to name my first daughter Vanessa Junior.

Vanessa: Why Vanessa Junior? Why not just Vanessa?

Me: I love the name so much I want to get married to a girl called Vanessa.

Vanessa: So, you are going to go about looking for a girl named Vanessa before you can get married. What if you don't find any?

Me: I pray I'll find one. If I don't at least I already know one.

Vanessa: Who ?

Me: The one I'm talking to.

Vanessa: (laughing out loud) You can't be serious. I'm not going to marry you.

Me: Why? You are going to break my heart.

Vanessa: You are so stupid.(she hits me softly)

What you are trying to do here is to see if this girl has any real interest in you, because if she doesn't, you might be wasting your time. If she interested in you, she'll become open with you, the next time you see her there'll be this glow in her face or excitement of being around you. A good way to know she's not interested is if she ignores all your advances. All most any girl will fall under you spell if you can get them to feel great. If she can muster up the courage to withstand all your sweet talking, my friend move on, she's not into you.

When I met Vanessa again, I asked her to go out with me. I can do this easily because she now sees her as my friend. She feels secure talking to me. Again I didn't do it directly. I told her that I felt bored and would like to go to some place to have fun. Girls love fun. I asked her if she will like to come along. Why not, she even suggested some place we could go. Even some that were beyond my budget, I gave her some made up excuses why I didn't like such places. Ultimately we agreed on a place to go and the rest is history. Sincerely, the name is no different from other names I've heard. I just used the name as a decoy to tell her I'm interested in her. If someone likes something as ordinary as your name, I don't see any reason why they won't like you also. From what I did. I tried not sound desperate. Someone desperate will try to get her number immediately or go ahead and say I love you or can we go out on a date which is a big no. Girls like to be teased, they enjoy fantasy, and if you can help them to build that fantasy, trust me, any girl will be yours.

There are a plethora of ways you can talk to girls and ask them out indirectly. Like sometime ago when I did my internship. There was this girl I worked with in my department. I wasn't that attracted to her. The job we did brought us together and we talked a lot about those things young girls like to talk about. Things like how some guys guys keep stalking her, how guys are bad and like to break a girls heart, the type of man she wants to be with etc. One day we were just talking and she told me that the girl I'm going to marry will be a very lucky girl. I was flattered. I thought what is so special about me that the girl who would marry be be very lucky? Well she just told me that she liked me indirectly. If she thinks the girl that would marry me would be very lucky, that translates to I am a special person to her. I'm found of using words to get girls to bring down their guard, but to what she just said I had no answer, she had beaten me in my own game. Before I could ask her out on a date, she said yes. Well you could say I did it officially and maybe she did it informally by nudging me in the direction she wanted to go. She didn't just beat me in my own game, but she has also given me a formidable weapon I could use in the future.

Code for the indirect method: Look for something about her other than her physical beauty to praise. It could be her name, her work ethic, her smile, her life style, her eyes. None of these things have to be special in any way. It is just a means to an end. For me there was nothing special about the name Vanessa. But saying I liked it got me to my destination. You can also praise her beauty. Look for ways to tell her she is beautiful without using the sentence "you are beautiful". Hearing it in many different ways turns her on.

CHAPTER 7

GETTING HER NUMBER AND THINGS TO AVOID SAYING

If you meet her for the first time and she responded positively to your conversation, collect her number by all means if you think your not going to meet her again. If she feels like, she'd give you even if she has no romantic interest in you. Remember your first discussion should not be you asking her out. It should be about getting to know her and building a rapport with her. If you've had conversation with her and you've become her friend, getting her number shouldn't be too hard. In fact if you don't ask for it in the first few weeks she will be the one trying to give it to you or even collect yours. When it's hard is when you feel you haven't really connected yet and you need her number so you can talk more.

BENJAMIN FRANKLIN TECHNIQUE

The Benjamin Franklin technique is a method he used to turn an enemy into a friend and later a strong supporter. I'm not going to be repeating it here, you can easily find it on Google. The Benjamin Franklin technique is easier to pull off If you work together, school together or you are in a group like choir, dance etc. Look for excuses like maybe burrow her note or text book and offer to call her so you can return it on time. You can get her number through this method if you are involved in any shared activity. I met a girl I had been trying to talk to in my neighborhood taking pictures with her friends. I told them they looked great and offered to join them. They laughed but I saw from their faces that they feel awkward allowing some unknown neighbor join them in their photo. Since they didn't like the first offer I made them another offer- to snap both of them together which they obviously cannot do by themselves. I told them they were so beautiful I would love to have their pictures on my phone (some flirting wouldn't hurt). They were already feeling great from the sweet words I was telling them. They allowed me to snap them with my phone. I offered to transfer it to them online through WhatsApp. They agreed and that was how I got her phone number(actually their phone numbers).

Burrowing things from her can often start a relationship where you can also offer to assist her with things she doesn't have. I know some guys who had to pretend they couldn't do an assignment just so that a girl they like could teach them. And when you get her number please do not text her. The beginning of a relationship is an opportunity to make a big impression on her and you can't do that by texting. When you feel you already have her, you can start texting her, otherwise you'd be giving yourself unnecessary stress. The problem with texting is that you can't really say much and you might find it difficult to express yourself. It's not just what you say that's important, how you say it is even more important. There's a way you'd say darling and someone would get turned on and there a way you'd say it and it wouldn't mean anything. When you meet someone you are attracted to, years of evolution comes to play their role for you- your face, your hormones, your voice and virtually everything about you tries to present the best version of you to that person. That's why you should call her, so she can hear your voice. And you should talk to her like someone in love. I've being with some guys that have mastered the art, even some bad guys with scary voice. When I hear them talking to their girlfriend on the phone, it's as if they are singing a melody. They talk softly and slowly, as if they can do no harm and they have everything in control. Girls find this very attractive. The good news is that you can easily learn it. Almost all guys already have deep voice, all you need is to polish it by talking quietly, slowly and softly. You need confidence to do this and that's what the first part of this book is about. If you lack confidence, it can easily show in your voice.

THINGS TO AVOID WHEN HAVING CONVERSATION WITH HER

While words might be the way to a girl's heart, there are certain words that could be a turn off and you should avoid when having conversations with her.

1. DO NOT BRAG ABOUT YOUR SELF

Do not make the relationship seem all about you. The easiest way to annoyed a girl is by bragging about how much money you have, the places you've been to, your latest Lamborghini etc. All of which might be big lies made up by you. From my experience people who have all these things are either tired of bragging about it or do not feel the need at all. Let her discover for herself what you are. You become even more sexy and attractive when she discovers through her friends or by chance that you have something special like car, house, money etc.

2. DO NOT ASK PERSONAL QUESTIONS IN YOUR FIRST CONVERSATION

It might make you seem desperate and she might not be comfortable having conversation with someone she barely knows.

Your first conversation should not be about knowing each other but not on a personal level. You shouldn't ask her if she's dating in your first conversation, except if you are Cassanova. I guess even Cassanova wouldn't do that. Asking questions like what are your goals in life or other things that might be for friends or intimate partner is a huge turn off.

Asking personal question on your first conversation will get them annoyed and feeling like you are intruding into their privacy. In your first conversation you should try to ask open ended questions about them that are not personal. Since people are happy to talk about themselves, tell a little about yourself and ask her open ended questions about herself. If you met her at work or in school, church, or any group, chances are that you already have a lot in common to talk about. Even some harmless gossip can do the trick, if you feel like going that way.

3. DON'T JUST TALK, LISTEN TO HER.

Sometimes a girl just need someone to share her heart with. Always resist the temptation to offer her advice. Girls want someone who will listen to them and show they care and not someone to advise them and tell them how to live their lives. Only offer your advice if she asks for it.

4. DO NOT TALK ABOUT ARCANE TOPICS.

Find out what interests her and what she likes to talk about. There are some topics that are universal that are not personal e.g. where you'd like to travel to and movies. To have more things to say you have to be cultured. This especially true for those STEM guys. If the only thing you want to talk about is some heavenly equations and some philosophical debates on the origin of man then you are going to have a hard time talking to many people, how much more girls. There are some topics such as politics or sports that guys enjoy talking about that will bore girls. The trick to having conversations and making connection with girls is to talk about what they are interested in. And if you are good at small talk, you are on the right path. Girls are mostly interested in talking about relationships, movies, gossips, shopping or travel experience and if you hear he singing music will be a good topic to discuss with her.

5. AVOID THE TEMPTATION TO JUDGE HER

The guy who makes her feel safe is the guy who will get her. Humans are a bunch of pretensionists. We can do something in private and judged others who are caught doing it. Actually we can't help ourselves, we were programmed that way. You do not just see a car, you see a red, black, old, new, cool or ugly car. But when it comes to relationship you have to throw away those tendencies. Girls like to be with guys with whom they are free to go wild with without being judged. She likes to feel you will not judge her if she asks for something risque. And you can do that by initiating such conversations. Talking dirty is one of the most sexy quality but they will not tell you. If they talk dirty you should encourage them. If they say something you find strange, take time to absorb what they're saying instead of reacting immediately. Make her feel safe by assuring her you will not judge her for being herself.

6. TRY NOT TO ARGUE WITH THEM.

You can disagree with them but avoid the temptation of trying to win argument when discussing with them like you do with your buddies. Most women avoid argument like plaque. Argument will turn a normal discussion in a competitive sport or a court case. Even if they know that you are right they don't care. They don't just like the feeling of loosing an argument. That's why women are always right even when they are wrong. A good way to end a conversation with a girl very quickly is to turn it into an argument. This is not what you want or what you should want. You want to spend as much time as possible with her getting to know her and making her more comfortable with you which will increase her attraction for you.

CHAPTER 8

MAKING USE OF THE SIGNS OF ATTRACTION

If you've molded yourself into the kind of guy that girls like, you'll begin to get green light from many girls. From smile to some lustful stare to even cold looks. The good news is that evolution has done a lot of work for you when it comes to attracting the opposite sex. Take some time out and thank Mr. Evolution. He understands your problem and that's why he designed some subtle signals people can use to find a mate and keep the species extant.

If a girl likes you, she wouldn't walk up to you and let you know. Social expectations, fear or rejection and many other things will prevent her from doing it. But, they've got some powerful weapons in their arsenal they can use to get a guy they like. These weapons are in the form of subconscious signs, although they can be sometimes cautious and deliberate. Many guys get rejected because they go for the wrong girls or they go at the wrong time- when she has not yet developed interest. If rejection is a big deal for you, then you are better off going for girls that are already interested in you. And how do you know they are interested? They give you signs.

SO WHAT ARE THOSE SIGNS THAT A GIRL LIKES YOU

Now a girl might really like you and being into you and yet might still not want to have a relationship with you. This might happen because of religious beliefs or she might not be ready to commit into any relationship at that point in time. It's not a must that someone that likes you will go into a relationship with you. I have left out some that are too difficult to observe or gives confusing signals.

THE TYPE OF SMILE

If she likes you you'll find her smiling at at you many times. But the fact that a girl smiles at you doesn't mean she likes you. It depends on the context. If she's a cashier, chances are she's smiling as a part of her job. I've found that the smiles that indicates love is often subtle and not very open and involuntary. She smiles and it quickly fades or she turns her face away from you so you won't catch her. Just like most of them will not come out openly to say they love you, they will not smile openly unless you are their friend or you are talking to them. It doesn't have to be a smile. Sometimes you just see this glow on her face that makes her look totally different and irresistible. In some people you will notice flushed cheek.That is every hormone in her body working together to tell you she finds you attractive. And you should believe it.

THEY FROWN

You see a girl and she gives you a weird look

for no reason. I used to think that maybe these girls have natural hate for me. I've come to discover it's a ploy to get your attention. We remember negative emotions more than positive ones. This will happen in particular if you are not paying attention to her, as they think they deserve your attention. I found this particularly true with girls that are older than I am, as is often the case I'm not interested in them(though not because I do not find them attractive). And in many cases the ploy has worked, I find myself thinking about why some person I have nothing to do with will be giving me such a weird look. I've dated some and for some other we just became friend.

SHE STANDS OR SITS IN A GROUP WITH HER BODY OR LEGS POINTING AT YOU

If someone does this it might be as a result of the person liking what they see and are trying to place themselves in a position to see more. Sometimes its deliberate and sometimes its subconscious. If you are in a group she would like to stand or sit directly opposite you. This happens so we can get a good view of the person we like.

SHE TEASES YOU

If both of you have gotten to know each other to an extent and she's comfortable talking to you, you might find her making some sarcastic comments about you or teasing you. She might be doing this to find out if you have a sense of humor and do not take your self too seriously. If she really likes you, she'll apologize if she thinks it got you annoyed.

SHE FINDS EXCUSE TO COME AROUND YOU

We like being close to the person we are attracted to. If someone likes you they'll want to see you more often and maybe get a chance to talk more with you. Sometimes she might give you some mudane task to do. They usually do this just to get close to you.

They'll ask you to help them out with some task that they can obviously do themselves. For example they might ask you to help them button the sleeves of their shirt or to do an assignment that a two year old kid could probably do. It's not about the task, it's about you coming close to them. This is in a way a type of flirting. They are looking for excuses to touch you.

SHE GETS CAUTIOUS OF HER DRESSING AROUND YOU

If she's always making adjustments to her clothing around you, she might like you and wants to present the best version of herself to you.

SHE TELLS HER FRIENDS ABOUT YOU

If a girl likes you, she will almost always tell her friends about you. If she has a close friend that suddenly started giving you some questionable smile when you come across each other she probably has told her about you. Since she's not allowed to say anything about it she will just tell you by smiling.

SHE FLIRTS WITH YOU

Ladies are very subtle about their flirting. They can flirt with you and the person standing beside you might not know what is going on. One way they flirt is to get into your personal space. I have experience this in different ways. For example a girl wanting to fix her shoe came close to me, bent down to fix her shoes, she held my hand as a support with one hand and used the other hand to fix the shoe. In about 5 seconds she was done. There are one thousand and one ways she could have fixed the shoe without coming close or holding my hand as support. I was too carried away by the fact that she was very close, I would have offered to help her tie the lace of the shoes as a gentleman. This was a girl I had been talking to and she sounds uninterested or maybe impossible to get. I gave her some space because I thought she was uninterested in me or snubbing me. I replied in kind by flirting with her and she responded positively. I later dated her. Other ways to flirt is through light playful touching although you have to be careful about this. Some insecure girls can easily claim sexual harassment, even when what you touched was their shoulder or hand. These girls get very little attention and think that the only way to get attention is by claiming that every little touch or coming close to them is sexual harassment. From my experience before a hot and beautiful girl will claim sexual harassment you've actually gone too far. That's why is best way to flirt is by using words. No matter how dirty your words no one can accuse you of anything and the ones that are interested will be the first to touch you.

SHE LAUGHS AT YOUR JOKES

While getting married to a comedian is no guarantee of happiness, women find men who are funny very sexy. Being hilarious is at the top of the list for the quality women want in a man. But women do not just want a man who can make them laugh, they want a man who can laugh with them. That is a man who has a sense of humor. Life is full of difficulties and ups and downs and a guy who can make a girl laugh will lighten up the atmosphere and make life easier. It also means you are fun to be around. However a girl that is really into you will laugh at even your jokes that you think are not funny. Sometimes you might find out she is the only one that laughed. Some girls that like you will find everything you do funny even when you are serious and think its not funny. You don't have to worry they are just fascinated by you. You don't have to be Chris Rock or Kevin Hart to make a girl laugh. You can make fun out of anything that surrounds you. Girls that like you will laugh at almost any effort you put in to make a joke. However if you think your sense of humor needs some polishing it's not difficult to pull up. You can start by spending time with some funny people (it could be friends), reading funny books and watching stand up comedy. There are some words that are funny no matter how you say them. I learnt a lot about being funny by closely watching one of my uncles. He could make fun out of almost anything. It was through him that I discovered that the way you say a word could make it funny.

IT TAKES TIME

It's takes time to find out if these signs really mean anything. The fact that she smiled at you or gave you a weird look on any particular day doesn't mean anything. You have to see those signs consistently(Okay, maybe two or more times). Many of these signs are subtle and if you are not used to them you'll just brush them aside. She will be frustrated and you'll be frustrated too. Being able to notice these signs will do you a lot of good.

CHAPTER 9

WHERE TO MEET THESE GIRLS

Why is this a topic ? There are girls everywhere. You meet girls in the mall, on your way to work, and virtually everywhere. Girls might be everywhere but you cannot get girls everywhere. That's because it's not easy to make a connection with them everywhere. Unless rejection is a huge part of your diet, you don't want to talk to girls who see you as a stranger intruding on their life. Okay, this very attractive girl just walked by you, and you hurry up to talk with her and ask for her number, or ask for a date. Some few girls will agree, but what you'll get most times is an angry no, and get the f*ck off. Even if you have a very high end car, most girls will enjoy the ride and then say goodbye.

In business there one very important factor, its location, location, location. Location is also important for dating. That's because while we like to believe that opposite attracts, it's not always true. In fact people are attracted to more and find it easier to make a connection with people who are similar to themselves. It's easier to develop chemistry with someone who is similar to you, but not too similar otherwise people would be marrying their siblings or cousins. Here are some of the best places to meet girls and make a connection.

SCHOOLS

For most of us school is our first chance at social interaction. The urge to date starts very early. Earlier than our parents would like innocent kids to. Parents often forget that they were once kids and did not start feeling these emotions when they were 20 or 30. It began way earlier than that. School is a good place to get to meet with, interact, and make a lot of life long friends. Many people met their life partners in school. Most people start dating in high school and maybe take the relationship serious in college in hope of getting married. While going to college puts many people in a lot of debt that they find difficult to pay, dating and the fact that you get to meet a lot of people is one the reasons people are still willing to attend college. School is a good place to meet girls and there might be a lot more girls than boys in school except, of course in Engineering and Physics department in college where girls are as scarce as gold.

CHURCH

This is also a good place to meet a lot of girls, but is also a tricky place. That's because you get to hear a lot of sermons that discourages dating, unless dating with the intention to marry. But, despite those sermons people still do what they want to do. Except for a few priests, no one take those sermons seriously. Our biological drive is stronger than those sermons. If you join a group in the church, like choir, drama, etc. you'll get even more opportunities to not just meet, but to know more girls. Girls will know you better, and people that know you are more likely to be attracted to you and date you. If you have a talent that will be useful to the church do not hesitate to use it. If you become a Sunday school leader, choir leader or instrumentalist, good luck handling the number of girls fighting for your attention. Joining a group in the church, even if you are not really committed to it, gives you a chance to interact with more girls and possibly date them.

PARTIES

Attending a birthday or a social gathering event can be a good way to meet new people. Parties bring together people from all kind of places and background together. People who you wouldn't have gotten a chance to meet in life, you can meet at parties. People coming to these events, come with an expectation to meet new people and interact, as a result people loosen up the guard they put up in other places .Many people meet their life partners for the first time at parties.

NEIGHBORHOOD

Yeah, as a child the first people you get to meet, interact and play with are those in your neighborhood. You talk, you share things like toys and become friends. You visit each other. People who share the same neighborhood know and trust each other more. If you approach a girl in your neighborhood, you won't be approaching her as a stranger. She probably already knows you and it will be easier to make a connection.

PLACE OF WORK

After school, people spend most of their time in their place of work. And if you work in a large company or with a lot of people, you get a chance to meet people who you like and can go into a relationship with. I think its very easy for people to become emotionally attached in the work place. If you do a lot of work together, you share your problems with each other, you spend 40 plus hours with them every week emotions are going to get involved sooner or later. Don't ask why cheating is common in the work place? The people that spend a lot of time together began to develop emotions for each other. The more time you spend with someone the more you get to know that person and the more you get to like them. You become attracted to the people you spend a lot of time with. People can easily form connection in the work place as a result of spending a lot of time with each other which is made possible because of your work.

BARS AND CLUBS

Bars are meant for entertainment and enjoyment. It's a good place to meet a lot of people. The drinks, the music, the dance, the atmosphere are all pointing to romance. Most bars are set up that way, to be a place where people can find and make love. Is it casual fling or something more serious, you'll get all of them at the bar. Bars are also good places to find people who want short term or no strings attached relationship.

CHAPTER 10

OVERCOMING THE FEAR OF REJECTION

Rejection can be very painful But it is part of life. So is success, failure, happiness, sadness etc. Any girl that accepts you has probably rejected more than a dozen of other guys. If you were accepted it is because some other guys were rejected. You cannot totally avoid rejection, the more girls you want the more rejection you are probably going to get. But, you can greatly reduced the chance of she rejecting you. If rejection still prevents you from approaching girls, then it's likely you've not been with many or even any. If 3, 4, 5 girls have said yes to you, then I don't think you'd be afraid of rejection. Nothing succeeds like success. Your previous success gives you the confidence to go for another one.

However no matter how confident you are

too much rejection can shatter that confidence. It is important to note that girls themselves are death scared of rejection, most of them know how it feels like to be rejected, they do not go about celebrating the fact that they rejected a guy. If you get too much rejection you might be approaching them the wrong way, which we have discussed in the preceding chapters of part two. You can greatly reduce your chance of rejection by going for girls who already like you. This you know through the signs they give you. Also you can get them to develop feelings for you by the way you approach them, which we already discussed. However there are still some other things that will probably make a girl reject a guy. Knowing them will prevent some unnecessary heartache.

Let's look at what might make her reject you:

1. She already has a guy:

Before you walk up to a girl do your

homework, if you don't and it turns out she already has a guy or she's into a serious relationship, you'll have your self to blame if you get rejected. If you do your homework, you'll find out if she already has someone in her life. You can even find out from her directly by having conversations with her. Some guys like to ask girls directly, but I prefer doing it in a subtle way. Asking directly will begin to bring thoughts like; why is he asking, he might be interested in me- which, for me, is going to spoil the fun. Some girls have let me know that they are in a serious in the process of sweet talking them. You don't even have to go that far, if the boyfriend is important to them, he will always pop up in your conversations. However some girls are willing to date another guy even though they are in a serious relationship. If she's that type she will also let you know by how far she allows you to go when playing with her.

2. YOU ARE BEING SEEN WITH A PARTICULAR GIRL WHO SHE THINKS IS YOUR GIRLFRIEND

No one wants to be number two. If it seems someone is in your life who is not really there, clarify to them that no one is. Or if you like dating more than one girl at a time make sure you keep your other relationship secret from her. You might not be able to do this always and it might get to a time when she's going to find out. The moment she finds out that relationship is doomed. But it might be a little price to pay to date many girls at a time.

3. YOU BOTH DO NOT HAVE CHEMISTRY

This might be related to background, and this is why people are attracted to people who are similar to themselves. If after some time of knowing each other you still feel awkward around each other or your interest do not align, it's a sign the relationship won't work. If both of you are too different from each other it might lead to conflicting interest and goals. This will prevent both of you from getting to know each other which is a big obstacle to attraction.

4. SHE DOESN'T KNOW YOU AND THIS IS THE FIRST TIME SHE IS MEETING YOU

Yeah, if you just walk up to girls anywhere, maybe on the road or in the mall or in a strange location, you are setting yourself up for a heartbreak. Girls pretend a lot and enjoy being chased before they accept a guy. Because they don't want to look cheap they might likely reject you if its the first time they are meeting you. But the rejection might not be because they are not interested, it might be that they feel the setting is not right. Sometimes you won't be able to find any reason for the rejection. You just have to move on.

Start building your confidence by talking to the girls who you have little romantic interest for. Flirt with them and tease them and watch how they react. Tell her subtly how special she is. Fill her mind with fantasies about love. Before long she will reciprocate. Or if she doesn't, you didn't have a strong interest in the first place. Lowering the stakes can actually help you build your confidence before you go for the real thing.

The more familiar a girl is with you, the less likely she is to reject you. That's why asking a girl out the first time you meet her is going to bring a lot of rejection. The best way to avoid rejection is to make a connection with her through communication several times and to look for signs that she likes you. If girls like you and you make some effort to let them know subtly, you'll get to know because you'll feel good around them. They'll match your energy. If they ignore all your subtle advances, son move on. If a girl ignores all my move it's a big turn off for me. I think she's either arrogant or full of her self or ultimately she doesn't want to have anything to do with me. The moment I know she doesn't like me my love for her seems to diminish or disappear. If I still like her, then what I'm really experiencing is lust and not love.

CONCLUSION

If you follow all the steps mentioned in this book, getting a girlfriend should be a challenge for you. The methods are not difficult to put into action and its even fun doing it. Knowledge is power only when you make use of it. It will take a little bit of time to ease into the methods, but as time goes on it will become like a second nature.Make use of the knowledge you have today and see a lot of girls flocking to you.

Like this book?

Let others know by reviewing it on Amazon.
Click on this link https://amzn.to/2OYERcG

Printed in Great Britain
by Amazon